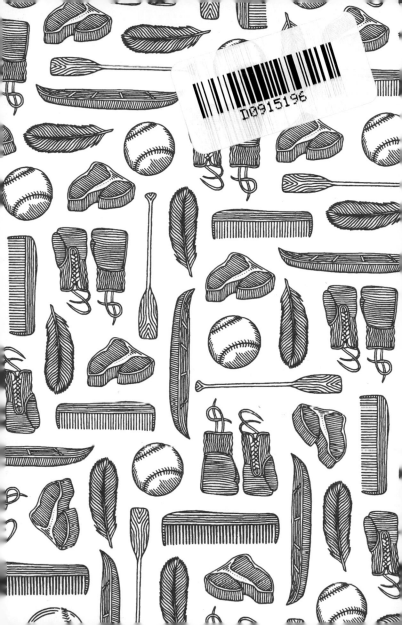

D0915196

WALT WHITMAN'S

GUIDE TO
MANLY
HEALTH
& TRAINING

WALT WHITMAN'S

GUIDE TO
MANLY
HEALTH
& TRAINING

ILLUSTRATED BY MATTHEW ALLEN

TEN SPEED PRESS
California | New York

CONTENTS

FOREWORD 3
INTRODUCTION 4

 1 THE VALUE OF TRAINING 6

 **2** GENERAL HEALTH & GOOD HABITS 22

 3 EXERCISE & SPORT 38

 4 GROOMING & DRESS 56

 5 FOOD & DRINK 74

 6 MENTAL HEALTH & MORAL FORTITUDE 88

 **7** MISCELLANY 104

CONCLUSION 119
ABOUT THE AUTHOR 123

FOREWORD

The following text, comprising of advice and musings from famed American poet Walt Whitman, was adapted from a series of 1858 newspaper columns he wrote under the pseudonym Mose Velsor. The columns—entitled "Manly Health and Training, with Off-Hand Hints Towards Their Conditions"—ran in the relatively obscure paper *The New York Atlas*, and were unknown to be penned by Whitman for over 150 years. The 47,000-word series was published after the first two editions of Whitman's famed *Leaves of Grass* had debuted to little fanfare, and before the landmark 1860 edition was published.

INTRODUCTION

ON
MANLY HEALTH

Manly health! Is there not a kind of charm—a fascinating magic in the words? We fancy we see the look with which the phrase is met by many a young man, strong, alert, vigorous, whose mind has always felt, but never formed in words, the ambition to attain to the perfection of his bodily powers—has realized to himself that all other goods of existence would hardly be goods, in comparison with a perfect body, perfect blood—no morbid humors, no weakness, no impotency or deficiency or bad stuff in him; but all running over with animation and ardor, all marked by herculean strength, suppleness, a clear complexion, and the rich results (which follow such causes) of a laughing voice, a merry song morn and night, a sparkling eye, and an ever-happy soul! To such a young man—to all who read these lines—let us, with rapid pen, sketch some of the requisites toward this condition of sound health we talk of—a condition, we wish it distinctly understood, far easier to attain than is generally supposed; and which, even to many of those long wrenched by bad habits or by illness, must not be despaired of, but perseveringly striven for, as, in reason, probable and almost certain yet to attain.

1 | THE VALUE OF TRAINING

ON
WHAT
TRAINING
ENTAILS

Training!
In its full sense, it involves

the entire science of manly excellence,
education, beauty, and vigor

—nor is it without intimate bearings
upon the moral and intellectual nature.

There is even no hunter, warrior, wild Indian, or the strongest and supplest backwoodsman of the West, but would have all his natural qualities increased far beyond what they are, by judicious training. This is art, the province of which is to take natural germs or gifts, and bring them out in the fullest and best way.

ON
THE ART
OF TRAINING

ON
THE GOAL
OF TRAINING

In robust training for this life, which is itself a continual fight with some form of adversary or other, the aim should be *to form that solid and adamantine fiber which will endure long and serious attacks upon it,* and come out unharmed from them, rather than the ability to perform sudden and brilliant feats, which often exhaust the powers in show, without doing any substantial good.

II

No amount of cultivation, intellect, or wealth, will ever make up to a community for the lack of *manly muscle, ability and pluck.*

ON
PLUCK

ON
REJECTING A
SEDENTARY LIFE

To you, clerk, literary man, sedentary person, man of fortune, idler . . .

Up!

The world (perhaps you now look upon it with pallid and disgusted eyes) is full of zest and beauty for you, if you approach it in the right spirit!

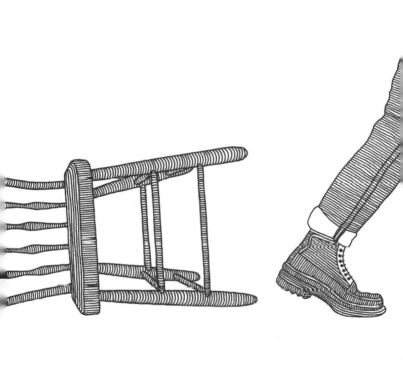

ON
STRENGTH
AND SIZE

Great strength may reside in persons
of ordinary general size, and is often
to be found there. Good parentage is
a great thing; but training, and proper
and systematic exercise, are also capable
of bringing out strength to a very great
degree, in those who have not inherited it.

With perfect health, (and regular agreeable occupation), there are no low spirits, and cannot be. A man realizes the old myth of the poets; he is a god walking the earth. He not only feels new powers in himself—he sees new beauties everywhere. His faculties, his eyesight, his hearing, all acquire superior capacity to give him pleasure. Indeed, merely to move is a pleasure; the play of the limbs in motion is enough. To breathe, to eat and drink the simplest food, out-vie the most costly of previous enjoyments.

ON
THE SPIRIT OF THE
HEALTHY MAN

Guard your manly power,
your health and strength,
from all hurts and violations
—this is the most sacred
charge you will ever have
in your keeping.

ON
GUARDING ONE'S
MANLY POWER

ON
THE MAN
WHO TRAINS

For he who once gets started, fully
awakened to the precious endowment
he has in his own body, beyond all other
wealth that can be acquired by man,
will not cease his interest in the subject,
but will go on toward a greater and
greater degree of inquiry, knowledge,
and perfection.

The observance of the laws of manly training, duly followed, can utterly rout and do away with the curse of a depressed mind, melancholy, "ennui," which now, in more than half the men of America, blights a large portion of the days of their existence.

ON
TRAINING
AND ENNUI

ON
TRAINING

[Training is] the magic word that can
remedy all the troubles and accomplish
all the wonders of human physique.

For, say what we may of the pleasures of the world, and of what is heroic, it comes down to this—that there can be no first-rate heroism except in a sound body, and that there really can be no gratification or pleasure, however costly, however much vaunted or rare, or sought for, that is equal to the delicious feeling, all through middle-age, and even old age, of being perfectly well.

ON THE VALUE OF A SOUND BODY

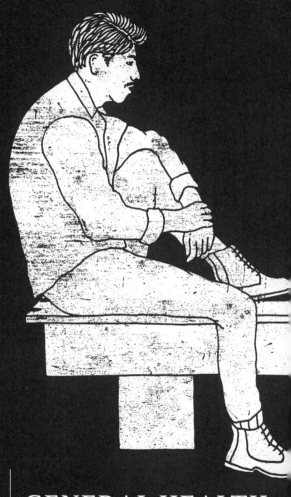

2 | GENERAL HEALTH & GOOD HABITS

ON
THE SIGNS
OF MANLY HEALTH

Among the signs of manly health and
perfect physique, internal and external,
are a clear eye, a transparent and perhaps
embrowned complexion (this latter not
necessarily), an upright attitude, a springy
step, a sweet breath, a ringing voice and
little or nothing of irritability in the temper.

Training, however, it is always to be borne in mind, does not consist in mere exercise. Equally important with that are the diet, drink, habits, sleep, etc. Bathing, the breathing of good air, and certain other requisites, are also not to be overlooked.

ON
GOOD HABITS

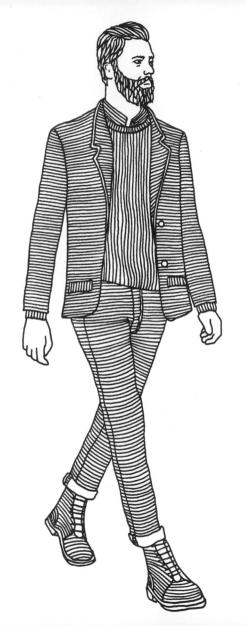

Always go with the head erect and breast expanded—always throwing open the play of the great vital organs, inhaling the good air into the throat, lungs and stomach, and giving tone to the whole system thereby.

ON
HOW A MAN
SHOULD WALK

ON
FRESH AIR

Few know what virtue there is in the open air. Beyond all charms or medications, it is what renews vitality, and, as much as the nightly sleep, keeps the system from wearing out and stagnating upon itself.

The healthy sleep—the breathing deep
and regular—the unbroken and profound
repose—the night as it passes soothing
and renewing the whole frame. Yes, nature
surely keeps her choicest blessings for the
slumber of health—and nothing short of
that can ever know what true sleep is.

ON
SLEEP

ON
BEDTIME
AND THE
BEDROOM

Ten o'clock at night ought to find a man in bed—for that will not afford him the time requisite for rest, if he rise betimes in the morning. The bedroom must not be small and close—that would go far toward spoiling all other observances and cares for health. It is important that the system should be clarified, through the inspiration and respiration, with a plentiful supply of good air, during the six, seven, or eight hours that are spent in sleep. During most of the year, the window must be kept partly open for this purpose.

ON
SOCIAL
RECREATION

The evenings ought to be devoted, to some extent at least, to friendly and social recreation, (not dissipation, remember). Friends may be visited, or some amusement, or a stroll in company—or any other means that will soothe and gratify the mind and the affections, friendship, etc.—for every man should pride himself on having such affections, and satisfying them, too.

[Training should be] a regular and
systematic thing through life. Not only
in young manhood, but in middle age,
and in advanced age, also, modified to
suit its appropriate requirements, should
the course of training be persevered in,
without intermission.

ON
TRAINING
THROUGHOUT
ONE'S LIFE

ON
TRAVEL

Often, a complete change of scene, associations, companionship, habits, etc., is the best thing that can be done for a man's health, (and the change is perhaps beneficial to a further extent in his morals, knowledge, etc.).

ON
THE HABITS
& REWARDS
OF A GOOD LIFE

Early rising, early to bed, exercise, plain food,
thorough and persevering continuance in gently-
commenced training, the cultivation with resolute
will of a cheerful temper, the society of friends
and a certain number of hours spent every day in
regular employment—these, we say, simple as they
are, are enough to revolutionize life, and change it
from a scene of gloom, feebleness, and irresolution,
into life indeed, as becomes such a universe as this,

full of all the essential means of happiness, full of well-intentioned and affectionate men and women, with the beneficent processes of nature always at work, the sun shining, the flowers blooming, the crops growing, the waters running, with all else that is wanted, only that man should be rightly toned to partake of the universal strength and joy. This he must do through reason, knowledge and exercise—in short, through training; for that is the sum of all.

3 | EXERCISE & SPORT

ON
WHERE
TO TRAIN

Places of training, and all for gymnastic exercises, should be in the open air—upon the turf or sand is best.

Cellars and low-roofed attics are to be condemned, especially the former.

[A man] who is devoting his attention . . .
to the establishment of health and a manly
physique, will do well to spend an hour of
the forenoon (say from 10 to 11 o'clock) in
some good exercises for the arms, hands,
breast, spine, shoulders, and waist; the
dumb-bells, sparring, or a vigorous attack
on the sand-bags, (a large bag, filled with
sand, and suspended in such a position
that it can be conveniently struck with the
fists). This should be done systematically,
and gradually increased upon making the
exertion harder and harder.

ON
DAILY TRAINING

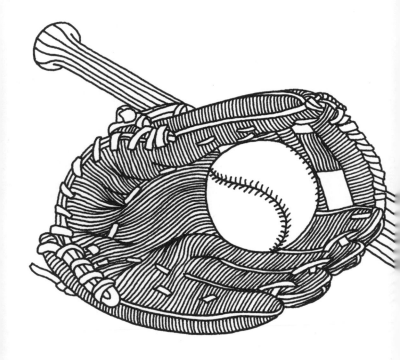

The game of base-ball, now very generally
practiced, is one of the very best of out-
door exercises; the same may be said of
cricket—and, in short, of all games which
involve the using of the arms and legs.

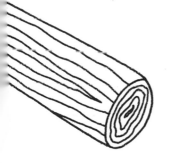

ON
BASEBALL

ON
ROWING

Rowing is a noble and manly exercise;
it develops the whole of the body.

Walking, or some form of it, is nature's great exercise—so far ahead of all others as to make them of no account in comparison.

ON
WALKING

Persons habituated to a daily summer swim, or to the rapid wash with cold water over the whole body in the water, are far less liable to sudden colds, inflammatory diseases, or to the suffering of chronic complaints. The skin, one of the great inlets of disease, becomes tough and thick, and the processes of life are carried on with much more vigor. Then cleanliness and enjoyment are also to be added to the merits of swimming.

ON SWIMMING

ON
TRAINING
THE LEGS

A great deal may be done by gymnastic exercises to increase the flexibility and muscular power of the legs. The ordinary exercise of bending forward and touching the toes with the tips of the fingers, keeping the knees straight meanwhile, is a very good one, and may be kept on with, in moderation at a time, for years and years. The simple exercise of standing on one foot and lowering so as to touch the bent knee of the other leg to the ground, and then rising again on the first foot, is also a good one. On the exercise ground, a good result is obtained from having a large stone and pushing or rolling it over, first by one foot, and then by the other, as long as it can be done without fatigue.

ON
BOXING

Is there not even a high order of heroism
in the willingness and capacity to endure
the most terrible blows of an opponent,
and stand up under them as long as the
sinews of the body answer the volition
of the mind?

ON
THE EXERCISE ONE
CAN DO ANYWHERE

To toss a stone in the air from one hand and catch it in the other as you walk along, for half an hour or an hour at a stretch—to push and roll over, a similar length of time, some small rock with the foot, thus developing the strength of the knees and the ankles and muscles of the calf—to throw forward the arms, with vigorous motion, and then extend them or lift them upward—to pummel some imaginary foe, with stroke after stroke from the doubled fists, given with a will—to place the body in position occasionally, for a moment, with all the sinews of the arms and legs strained to their utmost tension—to take very long strides rapidly forward, and then, more slowly and carefully, backward—to clap the palms of the

hands on the hips and simply jump straight up,
two or three minutes at a time—to stand on a hill
or shore and throw stones, sometimes horizontally,
sometimes perpendicularly—to spring over a fence,
and then back again, and then again and again—to
climb trees in the woods, or grip the low branches
with your hands and swing backward and forward—
to run, or rapidly walk, or skip or leap along—these,
and dozens more of simple contrivances, are at hand
for everyone—all good, all conducive to manly health,
dexterity, and development, and, for many, preferable
to the organized gymnasium, because they are not
restricted to place or time.

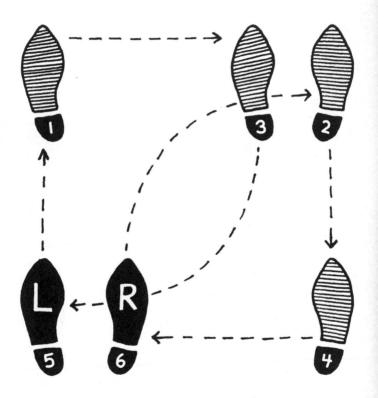

We recommend dancing, as worthy of attention, in a different manner from what use is generally made of that amusement; namely, as capable of being made a great help to develop the flexibility and strength of the hips, knees, muscles of the calf, ankles, and feet.

ON
DANCING

4 | GROOMING & DRESS

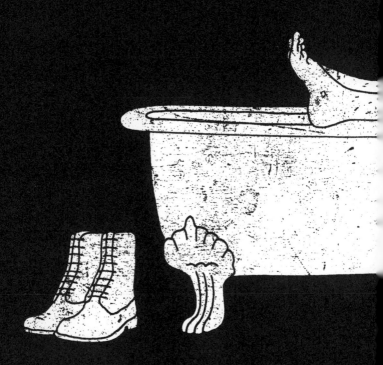

ON
A MAN'S IDEAL
MORNING ROUTINE

The man rises at day-break, or soon after—if in winter, rather before. In most cases the best thing he can commence the day with is a rapid wash of the whole body in cold water, using a sponge, or the hands rubbing the water over the body—and then coarse towels to rub dry with; after which, the hair gloves, the flesh-brush, or any thing handy, may be used, for friction, and to put the skin in a red glow all over . . . as soon as the glow is attained, the window, unless the weather is very bad, should be opened, and the door also, so that the room may become filled with good fresh air—for the play of the respiratory organs will be increased by the performances just mentioned, and it is at such times that good air tells best.

ON FASHION VS. FUNCTION

Of course, fashion must stand one side, if we are going to enter into the spirit of the thing seriously; *no man can serve the two masters, of frivolous fashion and the attainment of robust health and physique, at the same time.*

The tonic and sanitary effects of cold water are too precious to be foregone in some of their forms. You cannot have a manly soundness, unless the pores of the skin are kept open, and encouragement given to the insensible perspiration, which in a live man is thrown off in great quantities, and the free egress of which is of the utmost importance.

ON
COLD BATHS

ON
BEARDS

The beard is a great sanitary protection to the throat—for purposes of health it should always be worn, just as much as the hair of the head should be. Think what would be the result if the hair of the head should be carefully scraped off three or four times a week with the razor! Of course, the additional aches, neuralgias, colds, etc., would be immense. Well, it is just as bad with removing the natural protection of the neck; for nature indicates the necessity of that covering there, for full and sufficient reasons.

ON
SOCKS

The clothing of the feet is of importance; clean cotton socks in summer, and woolen in winter, carefully selected as to the size. These are little things, but on such little things much depends—yes, even the greatest results depend. And it is, perhaps, to be noted, that many a man who is mighty careful of his outside apparel—his visible coat, vest, neckcloth, jewelry, etc., is habitually careless of the fixings and condition of his feet.

Most of the usual fashionable boots
and shoes, which neither favor comfort,
nor health, nor the ease of walking, are
to be discarded. In favorable weather,
the shoe now specially worn by the
base-ball players would be a very good
improvement to be introduced for general
use. It should be carefully selected to the
shape of the foot, or, better still, made
from lasts modeled to the exact shape of
the wearer's feet (as all boots should be).

ON
SHOES

Probably there is no way to have good and easy boots or shoes, except to have lasts modeled exactly to the shape of the feet. This is well worth doing. Hundreds of times the cost of it are yearly spent in idle gratifications—while this, rightly looked upon, is indispensable to comfort and health.

ON
CUSTOM-MADE
BOOTS & SHOES

ON
SEASONAL
FOOT CARE

The feet, too, must be kept well clothed
with thin socks in summer, and woolen in
winter—and washed daily. We may mention
that one of the best remedies for cold feet
which many people are troubled with in
the winter, is bathing them frequently
in cold water. If this does not succeed,
add a little exercise.

The best rule is, instead of putting on all the clothing one can stand, to dress as lightly as is consistent with comfort, at the same time affording all parts of the body their requisite protection. The most prevalent error, of course, is too little protection about the feet, and too much about the head and neck. Since shaving has come in practice, (it ought to be scouted entirely from all northern countries), and since heavy mufflers, neck-winders, shawls, etc., have got to be generally used, all sorts of head and throat distempers have multiplied a hundredfold.

ON
DRESSING FOR
COLD WEATHER

ON
POST-EXERCISE
GROOMING

If the body is sweaty,
as it very likely will be,
it is best to strip,
rub down briskly with dry cloths,
and change the underclothes.

It is all in vain to pretend
that there is any real beauty,
or ever can be,
in a feeble or deficient man.

ON
THE FEEBLE MAN

ON
HANDSOMENESS

One ambition, at any rate, you ought to have . . . is the desire and determination to put your body in a healthy and sweet-blooded condition—to be a man, hearty, active, muscular, handsome—yes, handsome—for it is not for nothing that all through the human race there is the universal desire that the body should not only be well, but look well.

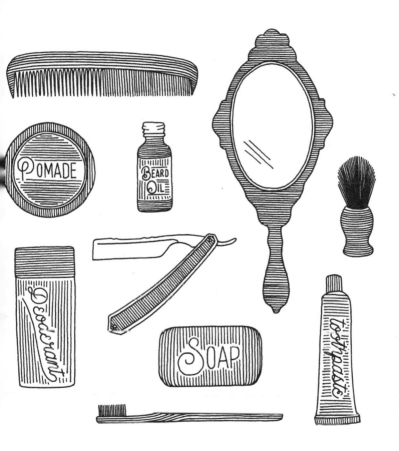

5 | FOOD & DRINK

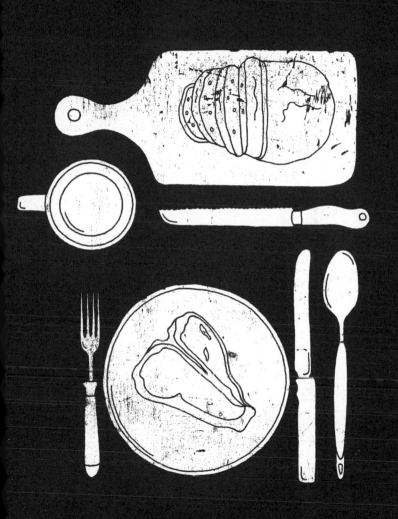

ON
THE THREE
DAILY MEALS

Usually the **BREAKFAST**, for a hearty man, might consist in a plate of fresh rare lean meat, without fat or gravy, a slice or chunk of bread, and, if desired, a cup of tea, which must be left till the last. If there be boiled potatoes, and one of them is desired, it may be permitted.

LUNCH should consist of a good plate of fresh meat, (rare lean beef, broiled or roast, is best) with as few outside condiments as possible.

The SUPPER, which must not be at a late hour, we would recommend always to be light—occasionally making this meal to consist of fruit, either fresh, during the middle and latter part of the summer—and of stewed fruit during the winter and spring.

ON
A HEARTY
MAN'S DIET

If you want to know what is best to
a hearty man, who takes plenty of
exercise and fresh air, and don't want
any pimples on his face or body, we
will answer (perhaps very much to your
astonishment), a simple diet of rare-
cooked beef, seasoned with a little salt,
and accompanied with stale bread or
sea-biscuit.

ON
DIGESTION

There can be no good health, or manly and muscular vigor to the system, without thorough and regular digestion.

Let the main part of the diet be meat, to the exclusion of all else. The result of this would be that the digestive organs would have more than half the labor (agonizing labor, it often is) withdrawn from them, and the blood relieved from an equally great amount of noxious deposit which, under the present system, is thrown into it.

ON
MEAT

ON
ALCOHOL

Very much of the violent crusade of modern times against brewed and distilled liquors is far from being warranted by the true theory of health, and of physiological laws, as long as those liquors are not partaken of in improper quantities and at injudicious times, disturbing the digestion. Of the two, indeed, we would rather, a little while after his dinner, a man should drink a glass of good ale or wine than one of those mixtures called "soda," or even a strong cup of hot coffee.

Eat enough, and when you eat that,

stop!

ON
NOT
OVEREATING

ON
HOW ONE
SHOULD EAT

Among the additional rules that may be mentioned
with regard to eating, are such as follow:

- Make the principal part of your meal always
  of one dish.

- Chew the food well, and do not eat fast.

- Wait until you feel a good appetite before
  eating—even if the regular hour for a meal
  has arrived.

- We have spoken against the use of the potato. It
  still remains to be said that if it agrees with you,
  and you are fond of it, it may be used; it is best
  properly boiled, at the morning meal. Do not
  partake of it, however, except in moderation.

- Drink very sparingly at each meal; better still
  not at all—only between meals, when thirsty.
  Any article craved by the appetite, and not of
  essential importance to be prohibited, may
  be allowed in moderation. This permission,
  however, does not extend to spirituous liquors.

- In general terms, avoid what disagrees with you; for there are, to every individual case, certain rules which apply to it alone. Study these, as they relate to your own case.

- There are even cases where a vegetarian diet applies. Such persons have an antipathy to eat meat. Of course, to them, it follows that they must eat what their appetite will permit, and what agrees with them.

- A cheerful and gay temper during and immediately after meals, is a great help to health.

- Never take any violent or strained exercise immediately after a meal.

ON
EVENING
REFRESHMENTS

A gentle and moderate refreshment at night is admissible enough; and, indeed, if accompanied with the convivial pleasure of friends, the cheerful song, or the excitement of company, and the wholesome stimulus of surrounding good fellowship, is every way to be commended.

6 | MENTAL HEALTH & MORAL FORTITUDE

ON
THE EFFECTS
OF TRAINING
ON CHARACTER

The results of properly chosen and well-continued courses of training are so valuable and so numerous that in mentioning them we would seem to be mentioning most of the precious treasures of character—among the rest may be specified courage, quickness of all the perceptions, full use of power, independence, fortitude, good nature, a hopeful and sunny temper, an industrious disposition, temperance in all the alimentative appetites, chastity, an aversion to artificial indulgences, easy manners without affectation, personal magnetism, and a certain silent eloquence of expression, and a general tendency to the wholesome virtues and to that moral uprightness which arises out of and is the counterpart to the physical.

The first requisite to a young man is
that he should be well and hardy;
and that from such a foundation alone,
he will be more apt to become good,
upright, friendly, and self-respected.

ON
CHARACTER
VIRTUES BORNE
OF HEALTH

ON
BODILY VIGOR
AND SUCCESS

Would you succeed in anything?—
ambitious projects, business, love? Then
cultivate this personal force, by persistent
regard to the laws of health and vigor.
And remember that the best successes
of life are the general resultant of all the
human attributes, expressed through a
fine physique.

Up in the morning early! Habituate yourself to the brisk walk in the fresh air—to the exercise of pulling the oar—and to the loud declamation upon the hills, or along the shore. Such are the means by which you can seize with treble grip upon all the puzzles and difficulties of your student life—whatever problems are presented to you in your books, or by your professors.

ON
EXERCISE FOR THE
SCHOLARLY MAN

ON
DEVELOPING BOTH
INTELLECT AND BODY

If you are a student, be also a student of
the body, a practiser of manly exercises,
realizing that a broad chest, a muscular
pair of arms, and two sinewy legs, will be
just as much credit to you, and stand you
in hand through your future life, equally
with your geometry, your history, your
classics, your law, medicine, or divinity.
Let nothing divert you from your duty to
your body.

ON INTELLECT AND LONGEVITY

True intellectual development,
not overstrained and morbid,
is highly favorable to long life,
and a noble physique.

What else, indeed, is the whole
system of training for physique, but
intellect applied to the bettering of
the form, the blood, the strength, the
life, of man?

ON
INTELLECT AND
TRAINING

ON MELANCHOLY

Brooding and all sorts of acrid thoughts, "the blues,"
and the varied train of depressed feelings, are among
the most serious enemies of a fine physique—while
the latter, in turn, possesses a marvelous power
of scattering all those unpleasant visitors, and
dissipating them to the winds . . . If the victim of
"the horrors" could but pluck up energy enough,
after turning the key of his door-lock, to strip off all

his clothes and give his whole body a stinging rub-
down with a flesh-brush till the skin becomes all
red and aglow—then, donning his clothes again,
take a long and brisk walk in the open air, expanding
the chest and inhaling plentiful supplies of the
health-giving element—ten to one but he would be
thoroughly cured of his depression, by this alone.

ON
MORAL
GOODNESS

A certain natural moral goodness is developed in proportion with a sound physical development.

A man must become . . . a reasoning
and reasonable being—must be willing
to follow a certain course, and find his
pay for the same, not in ephemeral and
immediate gratifications, but those at
some distance; must be willing to place
*health, sound internal organs, and perfect
condition, at the head of the list of the objects
of his whole life, here on earth.*

ON
A MAN'S VALUES

7 | MISCELLANY

ON
WHAT MAKES
A MAN HARDY

Storms, the cold, exposure, the sea, perils, enemies, war—all these, and the like of these, to superior and hardier spirits, instead of giving terror, give a certain sort of grim and manly delight.

The human frame is full, in every case, of latent power. Though wounded, buffeted, violated, time and again, it seems joyously to respond to the first return of reason and natural habitudes. Indeed, of all the amazing things about the human body, one of the most amusing is, how much it can stand, and still live on!

ON
THE HUMAN
BODY'S RESILIENCE

ON
TRAINING
THE VOICE

We would recommend every young man to select a few favorite poetical or other passages, of an animated description, and get in the habit of declaiming them, on all convenient occasions—especially when out upon the water, or by the sea-shore, or rambling over the hills on the country. Let him not be too timid or bashful about this, but throw himself into it with a will.

ON
HEALTH
AND WEALTH

From a money-making point of view . . .
health is an investment that pays better
than any other.

III

The really superb physique of man, involving his greatest heroism, faith, and unconquerable spirit of freedom, owes its birth and breed, not to the genial climes of this earth of ours, where the air is soft and equable, and fruits and perfumes run their even round the whole year, and where man has no effort to make for the support of his existence, but is permitted to lounge an indolent holiday of life, and dream it away in the poetic enjoyments of his appetites and amours—but to rougher and sturdier lands, where he has to fight hand-to-hand with the very earth, air, and sea.

ON
HARSH CLIMATES

ON
DOCTORS

Occasionally the advice of an intelligent and conscientious physician may be necessary—and such men are to be found yet. But, generally speaking, the benefit of medicine, or medical advice is very much overrated. Nature's medicines are simple food, nursing, air, rest, cheerful encouragement, and the like. The art of the surgeon is certain and determined— that of the physician is vague, and affords an easy cover to ignorance and quackery. The land is too full of poisonous medicines and incompetent doctors—the less you have to do with them the better.

A man that exhausts himself continually among women, is not fit to be, and cannot be, the father of sound and manly children. They will be puny and scrofulous—a torment to themselves and to those who have the charge of them.

ON SPENDING EXCESS TIME WITH WOMEN

ON
WORK

A steady and agreeable occupation is one of the most potent adjuncts and favorers of health and long life. The idler, without object, without definite direction, is very apt to brood himself into some moral or physical fever—and one is about as bad as the other.

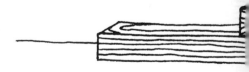

ON
MIDDLE AGE

The years of your middle age ought to be
those not only of your best performances,
but of your best appearance—and, if you
so will it, may be. Then all has become
ripe and mature; and surely the fully
ripened fruit or flower is no less beautiful
and welcome than any stage which
precedes it.

The periods of middle and old age are perhaps the finest, in some of the most important respects, through life . . .
*there is attainable a high flush condition
of stamina, strength, vigor, personality,
clearness and manly beauty and love-power,
thoroughly sustained many years, in perfect
specimens of trained health, through middle
and old age, towering in its ripeness and
completeness, till it rivals and fully equals
the best and handsomest specimens of early
manhood—and indeed transcends them!*

ON
OLD AGE

CONCLUSION

THE SURE REWARDS
OF TRAINING

To spring up in the morning with light feelings, and
the disposition to raise the voice in some cheerful
song—to feel a pleasure in going forth into the open
air, and in breathing it—to sit down to your food
with a keen relish for it—to pass forth, in business or
occupation, among men, without distrusting them,
but with a friendly feeling toward all, and finding the
same feeling returned to you—to be buoyant in all
your limbs and movements by the curious result of
perfect digestion (a feeling as if you could almost fly,
you are so light)—to have perfect command of your

arms, legs, etc., able to strike out, if occasion demand, or to walk long distances, or to endure great labor without exhaustion—to have year after year pass on and on, and still the same calm and equable state of all the organs, and of the temper and mentality—no wrenching pains of the nerves or joints—no pangs, returning again and again, through the sensitive head, or any of its parts—no blotched and disfigured complexion—no prematurely lame and halting gait— no tremulous shaking of the hand, unable to carry a glass of water to the mouth without spilling it—no film and bleared-red about the eyes, nor bad taste in the mouth, nor tainted breath from the stomach or gums—none of that dreary, sickening, unmanly lassitude, that, to so many men, fills up and curses what ought to be the best years of their lives, without good works to show for the same—but instead of such a living death, which (to make a terrible but true confession), so many lead, uncomfortably realizing, through their middle age, more than the distresses and bleak impressions of death, stretched out year after year, the result of early ignorance, imprudence, and want of wholesome training—instead of that, to find life one long holiday, labor a pleasure, the body a heaven, the earth a paradise, all the commonest habits ministering to delight—and to have this continued year after year, and old age even, when it arrives, bringing no change to the capacity for a high state of manly enjoyment—these are what we would put before you, reader, as a true picture, illustrating the whole drift of our remarks, the sum of all, the best answer to the heading of the two last sections of our articles, and the main object which every youth should have, in the beginning, from the time he starts out to reason and judge for himself.

ABOUT THE AUTHOR

WALT WHITMAN (1819–1892) was an American poet, essayist, and journalist whose work—including the seminal poetry collection *Leaves of Grass*—is some of the most important and influential of the American canon.

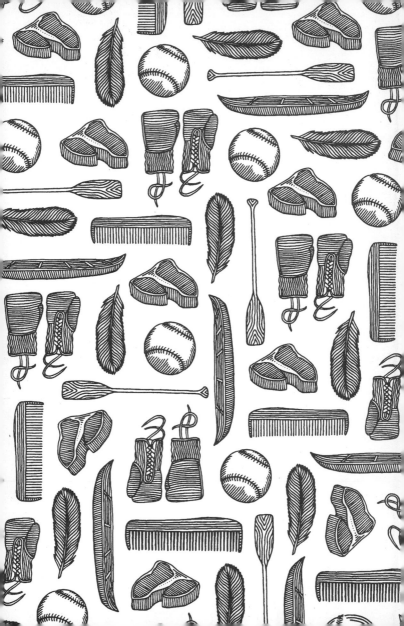